Young Ren pictured in the loving arms of his mother,
Sharon, in 2002.

To my Grandmother Wiika (Lea) and my late Grandfather, Ted.
Thank you for everything.

Editor: Lisa Frenette
ISBN: 9781778540387
For more book information go to https://medicinewheelpublishing.com
Printed in PRC
We acknowledge the support of the Canada Council for the Arts.
Published in Canada by Medicine Wheel Publishing.

# TEACHINGS OF THE DRUM

Ren Louie                    Karlene Harvey

Little Ren leaped out of bed at first light.
His cousins were coming—what a delight!

One cousin came in carrying a golden-brown drum.
Ren wanted to know what it was made from.

Grandmother said, "It's made from deer hide,"
"But what about the rim and the drumstick?" Ren pried.

"They're made of yellow cedar," Grandmother smiled,
"We call the drum a Cuká (koot-yuk)," she said to the child.

Ren and his cousins took turns with the drum,
while his grandmother began to sing and to hum.

Three years later when Ren turned nine,
his mom gave him a drum of her own design.

"Your heartbeat is what the drum sound stands for," Ren listened as his mother shared even more.

"Wrapping it in your arms to warm it is correct,
and placing it face up shows your drum respect."

Ren was so happy to have his own drum,
it was very special knowing where it came from.

Ren's love for singing and drumming grew fast,
at school he even drummed with his class.

No matter his fear of singing out loud,
Ren kept on drumming and began to feel proud.

Today, Ren shares the teachings he was told,
helping other children to be brave and bold.

He brings his favourite drum wherever he goes,
practicing his culture and sharing what he knows.

## Author

**Ren Louie** is Nuu-chah-nulth from Ahousaht and his traditional name is Wikinanish, which translates to 'eldest son'. He comes from mixed Nuu-chah-nulth, African American, and Ukrainian heritage. With his background in Indigenous Studies and his work as an Aboriginal Role Model in schools, he hopes to one day teach Indigenous Studies at the post-secondary level. Ren is passionate about his language and culture and enjoys learning new songs and traditional teachings from Elders and Knowledge Keepers in the Indigenous community. Born and raised on Lekwungen and WSÁNEĆ Territory in Victoria, B.C., Ren continues to live there today.

## Illustrator

**Karlene Harvey** is an illustrator and writer, and she lives on the unceded and ancestral home territories of the Musqueam, Squamish and Tsleil-Waututh people. She is Tŝilhqot'in through her mother and Syilx through her father, both sides of her family include a mix of European ancestry. Following her studies at Emily Carr Institute of Art and Design, she pursued an illustration practice that was inspired by zine and underground comic culture, independent animation and collage art. In recent years, she is invested in representation and how to best depict diverse peoples within her drawings. She recently completed a Master of Arts degree in English Literature with a specific focus on Indigenous literature at the University of British Columbia.

karleneharvey.com